THEIR PERF

by the same author

Changing Sides (Peterloo Poets, 1983)
Skedaddle (Peterloo Poets, 1987)

Their Perfect Lives

JOHN LEVETT

PETERLOO POETS

First published in 1994
by Peterloo Poets
2 Kelly Gardens, Calstock, Cornwall PL18 9SA, U.K.

**A catalogue record for this book is available
from the British Library**

ISBN 1-871471-41-9

Printed in Great Britain by
Latimer Trend & Company Ltd, Plymouth

ACKNOWLEDGEMENTS are due to the editors of the following journals and anthologies: *Encounter, The Guardian, London Magazine, London Review of Books, Literary Review, New Statesman, The Orange Dove of Fiji* (Hutchinson), *Orbis, Outposts, The Poetry Book Society Anthology 1989/90* (Hutchinson), *Poetry Durham, Poetry Now* (BBC Radio 3), *Poetry Matters, Poetry Review, Prospice* and the *Times Literary Supplement.*

"A Shrunken Head" was the joint-winner of the 1991 National Poetry Competition.

Contents

page

9   Am
10   The Gas-Mask
11   A Shrunken Head
12   Steam
13   Pomegranate
14   Zebra
15   So Smart
16   A Slip
17   Kippers
18   Nets
19   A Long Shot
20   Pluto's Fist
21   The Butterfly Centre
22   Greenhouse
23   Freeze
24   Calor Gas
25   Café
26   Stag
27   Stitches
28   Talc
29   Steps
30   A Wink
31   What's Sex Like?
32   Heirloom
33   Lullaby
34   A Yard of Chiffon
35   Pricking the Violet
36   Singeing
37   A Cigar
38   Airfix
39   Love and Kisses
40   Slush
41   Coconut
42   A Different Fireside
43   A Clean Shave

44 Early Warning
46 Soundtrack
47 Mascara
48 Vacuum
49 X-Ray

Am

The slightest words define the most.
Am, for instance, filling up a life,
Expressing, if expression is compelled,
The body's territorial extent;
Assertion's power to concentrate
A colony of egos in
Their dusty settlements of skin.
Denials, deprecations, steppings down,
Apologies like mornings, wry with mist,
Assumptions of uniqueness, leaky dawns,
Fluorescent, repetitious afternoons,
And fragile nights with sprays of stars,
Each chip and bit, each lucid smithereen,
A glimpse inside what might have been,
A looking-glass of overripe
And tinily declarative
Boltholes
Speckled with defections and
Disfigured with this spreading black
That takes each thinning drift of breath
And will not give it back.

The Gas-Mask

Its foetid tubes outlasted usefulness,
War issue circa 1939.
She let me put it on. No one would guess
The skull that filled the rubber snout was mine.
My voice, sucked down into the past decade
Through pipes and perished mouldings, sounded wrong,
Too hollow, other-worldly, too betrayed;
The noise I'd make if I had not been born.
The eyepieces were yellow, pickled cracks
Zigzagged into a musty nasal cave,
A shelter from the senseless dawn attacks
Of guilt and fear if I dared misbehave.
Anonymous I'd prowl the scullery,
Visit every room, patrol the stairs,
Sealed off from mustard-gas and Zyklon-B,
Dive-bombing beds, napalming rocking chairs.
The mirror in the hallway trapped my shape,
Half a face, a trunk, two rolling eyes,
The blind stare of some technocratic ape
At high-octane liana in the skies.
It grew too hot. My head stewed in my breath,
A sapping, unhygienic foetal bath;
I fought myself and died rehearsing death
Still strapped inside a face that couldn't laugh.
There comes a time when all pretending stops,
The door is opened, out you go to play,
You grab your mask, your bag of acid drops,
Then run and duck towards the grainy day.

A Shrunken Head

He's been stitched-up; two gummed, black-threaded eyes
Squint back across the decades in surprise
Through spiteful chinks of sunlight, acrid smoke,
Screwed-up against some wicked tribal joke.
His rictus has been sewn into a smile,
A tight-lipped dandy, puckered into style,
The clearing where his grisly fame began
Still broods beneath the kinks of wood-stained tan.
Flayed leather now, his features smoked and cured,
His niche in culture gruesomely secured,
The needled grin is fixed, drawn back and set
Bone-dry in its reflective cabinet.
A hundred years ago he strayed alone
Towards this room of ritual skin and bone,
Believed in spirits, drank, was secretive
With knives and fish-hooks, dreamed his seed would live,
Sheathed his penis, sweated half the night
On invocations, prayed, prepared to fight,
And felt, perhaps, the moon's leaf-parted shine
Move up his legs and bathe his severed spine;
His head hacked off, half-baked into this face
That swings and grins inside its airless case.
Hung-up, he seems to twitch at each dropped word,
As if, although we whisper, he had heard,
And stares through us to what we cannot see,
Our unstitched smiles, their pale atrocity.

Steam

Tipped up inside the gleaming room
Her wet hair streamed into the sink,
Warm water shed its snorkelled bloom
Onto her raw, responsive nape;
Dead lathers left her in the pink,
The bubbles made their charmed escape.

The whole scene was detachable.
Oatmeal and lemon, white and green,
The towel fluffed on the cork-topped stool,
The burst sachet, the malformed tube,
The three sides of wet polythene
That curtained the hygienic cube.

She turned and disappeared with steam
Into her freshly-opened pores,
Successive rinses briefly seamed
The camber of filmed porcelain
Then spiralled down to re-explore
The sponge's dumped, exotic brain.

Afterwards the place was light,
The heavy condensation gone,
The white-glazed tiles were watertight,
The mirror cleared, the shelves streamlined.
In a while, she'd said, perhaps she'd phone
Or write if she had half a mind.

Pomegranate

My grandmother had cut the thing in half
Then halves again, exposures we could share;
Each slice still glows, a neural photograph,
Uncovered membranes shimmer in cold air.
Aladdin's nightlights. Phoney power cells
In viral cubes so red they almost throb.
Interiorities. A shine that swells.
The first bloom on the neurosurgeon's swab.
That such an uninspired, lacklustre fruit
Could have this deranged beauty stashed inside;
The morning's ultra-red, hymenal loot
An optical surprise solidified.
I hid some pips inside my money-box,
Spoof jewellery that withered overnight;
Now, after thirty years, a morning rocks
This foetus bathed in dehydrated light.
Packed down into the bright squares of her shawl
She wets her lips and breaks into a grin.
Her white teeth slip; inflamed and glacial
The damaged gums beneath are glistening.

Zebra

One sniff would fur the throat,
Immobilize the tongue,
Sponge down the larynx, coat
The wind-pipe and the lung.
Its potency was caught
On fans of palsied air,
The morning a retort
That trembled over fire,
A curtain of cooked crêpe
And warm, narcotic steam,
Its lyrical escape
From hyperactive flame,
Or bronchial ascent
Above dim ropes and cones,
Night's heavy fender bent
By sodium's splintered bones.

First blacks then whites then blacks
The coarse strips alternate
Between the punched knick-knacks
Of aluminium plate,
Fish bowls of orange light
That flicker on their posts;
Look right, look left, look right,
A litany of ghosts.
In April he was killed;
They laid this down by May.
Municipally willed
He blinks there to this day
But cannot comprehend
His empty seat and desk,
Why, when he raised his hand,
The teacher never asked;
His pile of dust-filmed books,
Each bright, adhesive star
That lit his run towards
This whiff of burning tar.

So Smart

Onions, blind as gudgeon, nose and press
Against the acid murk that fills their jar,
A tarnished stare, unblinkered bitterness
Sealed up inside each souring cornea.
He twists the lid and air comes with a sob,
A suck, a bobbed commotion as they rise
And crowd the neck and, agitated, mob
The catch his fork and thumb extemporise.
Their perfect lives are over. From now on
Their uterine complexions will depend
On tiltings where the kitchen light has gone,
Its inexact and vinegary bend.
He captures one and puts it on her plate;
The layered skins immaculately shine
Then wink and pucker, shrink, evaporate,
So smart, she thinks, so stung they could be mine.

A Slip

The foothills of a cloudless sky
Have humped and powdered into dunes,
Their blue-flecked beaches treasured by
Half-buried cups, cheap tablespoons.
The washboard's slope of frosted spars
Swaps lathers as its glassed suds stream,
Pricked rainbows, soap-shagged reservoirs,
Pinked eyelids in a head of steam.
My mother's touch is rough, beneath
The scrubbed band of her wedding ring
A faint red itch, a rash so brief
It flares without her noticing:
The smoky party, drinks, a kiss
That sucked her through a locked back door
Past bundled coats, down stairs to this
Chilled basement's disinfected floor.
A slip. The foetus came and went
One dank, convected Friday night,
Left nothing but detergent, scent,
Sharp cheek-bones pocketing the light.
Time bleaches. Buttons plink and dry,
Cuffs wobble round their airless drum
Where whites and cottons flop and sigh
And gather for her hands to come.

Kippers

In candlelight their buffed Etruscan skins
Seem hollow and metallic, out of date,
Bronze aerosol on buckled near-side wings
Old dents from soft collisions decorate;
But closer to your surgery reveals
An orange flesh, a chemical conceit,
Each flank sunk in warm sepias of oil,
Stiff fans of tailbone spread against the heat.
You probe the moist clairvoyance of the spine,
Salt filaments your fork and fingers tease
And strip to saline whiskers pitched so fine
They tune into translucent frequencies,
Prick up and tingle, quiver with the flame,
Alive to airborne secrecies; a sigh
Grows tidal and ambiguous, your name
A roar the years between us amplify.
No word of mouth, no aerograms, no calls,
Your silence spits and hisses, jammed and faint,
A white noise in the candle as it trawls
For skin and bone as bright and cracked as paint.

Nets

They shroud domestic mysteries,
dusk's dumb-shows where the half-a-chance
we've waited half our lives for never comes.
Dim privacies, the bioluminescence of T.V.,
scorched daffodils, the white, narcotic twitch,
unsympathetic stitches, puffs and glooms,
and chunky clocks like cuff-links, antlered lights;
all floss spun from abstractions, love and thrift
in padded cells, soft sofas, glassy flames.

On cool spring nights, inflated like bibbed frogs,
you sometimes see their whiteness gathered in;
ringed hands emerge from closed suburban lives
still moist with soap and oestrogen or shrunk
to scentless parchments, forty years apart,
yet side by side down avenues and lanes
and hauling in their catch before it rains.

A Long Shot

for Peter

Lacking a dice my ingenious son
Has made a frail, six-sided paper one.
A lobotomized cube, its hunkered shape
Is sealed with twelve collars of sellotape
And decorated with twenty-one dots
Like orbital, lunar forget-me-nots.
He throws the dice for five, I roll a three
Astonished by its botched geometry,
Its bobbled spin, its solo hit and run
Through house dust turned galactic in the sun.
It lands askew, he gets down on his knees
To focus on the inked astronomies
And breathes in very slowly to address
This momentary perch of randomness;
Our carpet and our sofa that maroons
The hindered odds on six blue paper moons.

Pluto's Fist

My transfers never took, or not for long,
Saliva and cheap artwork peeling off
Or breaking on her saturated tongue
To flecks of Pluto's fist and Popeye's nose,
Acrylic tea-leaves, pointillistic froth,
Capillaries, pores doped with cellulose.

Her film of spit would glisten and then thin,
Exasperated colour basked and cooled
On tender strips of visionary skin;
She'd pull the tissue back and slowly tease
A fuzzy likeness, outlines crudely tooled
And proofed against our gobbed transparencies.

That term she met a boy with fake tattoos,
Mauve hearts, barbed arrows piercing LOVE and MUM,
A seethe of hypodermic reds and blues
That hung around all evening like bad news
And left, beneath a scent of bubblegum,
The ultra-violet rumour of a bruise.

The Butterfly Centre

for Ruth

Too pretty by half their chalks and flicked inks
Lift-off from gravel and circle the plants,
Up to their bright, barometric high-jinks,
Dodging down drinkable flightpaths of chance
To customize sunshine, flicker and lurch,
Vamp and soft-pedal, cant over and skim;
Taut, narcissistic, outspread to research
Each dickering paint-chart's unfixable whim:

Tranquillized lilacs, regressions of gold,
Haunted manillas and shoaled, nitrous blues,
Skeletal lemons, quick lacings of mould
Swallowtails sew by your black canvas shoes.
Their hand-woven gimmicks tickle the air
Grazing from pad to ephemeral pad
And leapfrogging ferns that scaffold the glare
To touch down on netting's trembled brocade.

Distracted you turn and crane over the pond
Where gnats refuel above urinous rocks
And crapulous goldfish decay with their blond
Submarine passions, your dazzled white socks
Stepping from childhood and onto a brink,
Steadied for something more solid and real
Than promises lit by these papery winks
Or the heat that inherits their vanished appeal.

Greenhouse

It's like walking through a sick lung:
spores, growths, respiratory damp,
ripe passages, declensions, soft dead-ends
and pulmonary cul-de-sacs;
ductfuls, emphysemic draughts
where cucumbers hang dreamy pricks
and, pressurized sophisticates,
the orchids ape rare blow-jobs in mid-air.
This feels like someone's future. Locked outside
ghost aerosols of autumn frost
smoke sniffily across a shaven lawn
where sprays of dew trick out their spritzed
freeze-dried instants unaware
of crippled seasons, Spring's coronary slur.
Beyond the polystyrene plots,
thermometers and thermostats,
the countryside has caught a cold;
moisture, resins, aphids, blight,
pine's decongestant, hazel's sneeze,
the oak's gnarled supplication, chilled and bare,
as England blows its snotty nose
and one more snuff of ozone goes
and leaves the willows weeping in despair.

Freeze

Someone, at least, has salvaged your grin
From the murk of the 60's 'available light'.
How old were you in those foundered jeans?
It looks so cold and far too late.
And where were you? Who drove you there?
It could be a garden but it's hard to tell.
And who took the picture? Was it his idea?
Were you always so willingly vulnerable?
You must have liked him, to grin like that,
Your third of a smile that first pulled me up,
But was he still there when it started to hurt
Or gone before you could jerk him awake?
And the cold is strange. You were never so white,
Never so candidly close to the bone;
This might be the back of a polar night
Or a twilit Finland, a targeted zone.
You would grow, of course, before we met,
But all the essentials were there in your face
Though I hadn't even imagined you yet
And was colder myself in another place.

Calor Gas

We camped out in your sister's flat,
Her low bed with its flat green sheets
And olive duvet piped with lime.
We stared up at the highly wrought
And conscientious ceiling that would take
Three coats at least to keep it white.
Her far from certain life lay round about;
Hair-sprays, make-up, capsized boots,
Two unwashed mugs with small red spots,
Her perfect strawberry bedside lamp
That lit its quarter of the room,
Steep china bowls of crisps, white rum;
Two docile glasses set down for
An imminent return.
After you made coffee and we sat
Cross-legged on the patterned floor
And thirsty from the heat chucked out
By the brand new silver fire;
Calor gas, thin mantles turning through
A brief, foreshortened spectrum,
White to red to blue.
We brought them two unopened packs
Of crisps and, as an afterthought,
Some liebfraumilch left tightly wrapped
In yellow tissue on the bed;
Our note of thanks beneath the keys,
Your punctual script in biro pointing out
Her one good bulb, the bedroom light, had blown.

Café

I watch you watch the coffee tread with milk
Through ochre into billowings of tan,
A cumulus as soluble as chalk
Around the plastic paddle of the spoon,
Then lighten to a fibre-optic blond,
A puzzled disc you indolently spin,
A settlement of cream one shade beyond
The half-light on your nineteen-carat skin.

I'm muddled. You're despondent. In the blue
Below your separate lashes I can see
The cup hung like a polystyrene clue
In neon's unpredictability:
I focus on your softly swinging shoe
Prepared to toe the line, or disagree.

Stag

The last thrill fades, the specialized
Nerve endings draw into their skins,
We come apart on giant-sized
Discourtesies and swollen grins;
The brackens wag, an airless heat
Inflates the veins that thread your feet.

I lift my belly and unscroll
The Durex with its ambushed sperm;
White dreams gone down the rabbit hole,
Dead embryos to keep us warm:
A handful of genetic slack
Runs down its screwed-up cul-de-sac.

Shifting camp the deer trek down
To see what's happened; as you turn
Their heads poke out and antlers crown
Cool looks of startled unconcern:
Impressionistic bushes yield
Soft heads on an impromptu shield.

They watch as we slide down the hill
With bags and camera, keys and shoes,
Outsize, discoloured, vulnerable,
Two sunlit backs a cloud pursues;
A month of dying grass and air
Supports their brown, corrective stare.

Tonight you'll lie in bed with him
Bruised and stung and sore inside
As sleep comes down and lets you climb
Into our freshly trampled hide,
And from its bushes, as you wake,
Imaginary horns will break.

Stitches

He's in there now, my big, depressive fish.
His luke-warm water jellies like a glue,
Decaying food and faeces smear the glass,
Tobacco burns his steel reflection blue.
March turns to April. Rain and cloud exult,
Their whistled extroversion cleans the air;
His chronic silence echoes like a bolt
Withdrawn and shot to let me know he's there.
He wants me now, I know, to go to him,
To scrape him down, hose off his silky gloom,
To show him with my cold hands how to swim
In self-deluding circles round the room.
How can I tell him? Is there really time
For love and exculpation? I must fly.
He'll rot, of course, go blind inside that slime,
But I'm so late, have other fish to fry,
Or one, at least, who's promised me the moon
In pockets of split tissue, soldered thirst;
Who fills me like some pink, stitch-strained balloon
Then holds me there until I almost burst.

Talc

He's buried in the garden, cutting logs,
His violet hands exhuming with the saw
Pale, anal rings, pine's sweetly opened cogs,
As sawdust floats in blond drifts to the floor.
The storm came overnight and ever since
He's lit up with this fever to dispose,
White knuckles barked with stains as sharp as quince,
Boots speckled with these vegetable snows.

He's high on it, the kick-start and the whine,
The trembled, oily mirage of its shape,
Heat's squeal as smoke and resins recombine
And shiver as the first tart spurts escape.
Knee-deep in roots and petrol rags he toys
With anchored blades, with feed-lines and choked links.
He's crashed out in a womb. One of the boys.
All night, between our sheets, the motor reeks.

He'll cut me up one day, I'm almost sure;
He sees these films and talks about my skin,
And when he's climbing on me he explores
Old seams and knots, he swears, where he'll begin.
It wasn't always like this. He was good,
Red fingers groped like coral, branched and shrunk;
Now lips are split, talc spills its powdered wood
In drifts against the stretch-marks on my trunk.

Steps

A warm pool, one blue flight
Laid flush into the stone,
Her foot's adhesive print,
The padded smudge of bone,
The white gap where her arch
Shrank back, the wave and feint
Of temperatures that parch
The damp's unstable paint.

All day the glass was fogged.
I watched her husband's eyes,
Suspicion waterlogged
Or sunk with ironies;
Her shadow's glossy bake
Stretched out across the grip
Of tiles that turned opaque
Like salt to crust her hip.

Last week he hit her twice
So now she simply sits
And tips and breaks the ice
Indifferently to bits;
Her blouse has come adrift,
Her footprints, as they dry,
Grow tinier and lift
Their body like a sigh.

A Wink

You left me, browsed along the aisle,
Then bent and tucked behind your ears
Blond hair that curtained off your smile
Above a tray of freckled pears
And apples in blue tissue, kale,
Its hairsprung formulations and
Its tight, fastidious detail
That oversimplified your hand.
Beside you swung red plastic nets
Of oranges and mandarins
And glandular, pumped-up courgettes
And onions' futuristic skins;
White parsnip, ginger's khaki prongs,
A mushroom's fanblade, mirrors where
Washed plums and peaches lounged among
Albino clouds of cauliflower.
The owner's hands were fat and thick
With earth and dirt beneath their nails,
He took your money with a wink
Then joked behind his dented scales;
I watched him eye you up and saw
The melons' halved, absorbent mouths
Grin back, like me, at shadow where
His fingers almost smudged your blouse.

What's Sex Like?

Our glad rags on the line
Inflate and clap their hands
As rain, like surplus wine,
Is barrelled in and lands
To fill the air with the pale see-through
Travesties of me and you.

My trousers and your skirt
Let rip and rock and roll,
They jig above the dirt
Then leap out of control;
I loose my legs, you sharply raise
Your hemline to its crotch of haze.

All night we've carried on,
Made all the deepest moves,
Now wind, like skin and bone,
Falls out of underclothes
As drenched seersucker lifts and stalls
On denim's phantom genitals;

Your tights wrap up my socks,
My vest slaps down your dress,
A cradled tee-shirt rocks
Its thermal emptiness,
And sleeves and cuffs rehearse their crude
Attempts at male solicitude.

'What's sex like for a bloke?'
Might as well ask the air
Inside these legs that poke
This space a blouse leaves bare,
Or stand and watch the bright brass zip
Eat up its blue, autistic hip.

Heirloom

His skin, a lustrous plastic in its case,
Is dry, too dry to ever leap again
Or surface in that dank, midge-ridden race
Recycled by decades of stippling rain.
The evenings made an heirloom of his eye,
Firelit, inquisitorial, agape
It glazed with antique memories, the fly,
The rod and line, the hook's barbaric shape,
And clouded with the turmoil of the catch,
The varnished scales articulate to feel
The whack and thrash, the taut, repeated snatch
And plunge that fed the epileptic reel;
The mist of resignation as it dried,
Not guessing in the chilled slump to the net
At life to come shut in this rarefied,
Blue-backed, fern-tangled, airtight cabinet.
The fisherman is dead. His sons are dead,
And their sons too, time's casual defeats;
A haemorrhage, some cancers, suicide,
Closed hospitals, a maze of bombed-out streets:
And still the pike lurks sideways in his gloom,
The tarnish of that flinching, sunlit day
Refloated as the lamplight in our room
Is tilted into dusk and pours away.

Lullaby

We picked our way with your plastic torch
through puddles shining down the lane
and sensed before we felt the smart,
transparent spits of rain,
and heard before we saw the sea,
its banked-up, blacked-out engine room
changing pitch and shifting gear
on a journey of its own;
and then stepped up and into
refrigerated skies
as the radar fanblades filtered out
white constellated noise,
and electronic castles
built on the unlit air
fortified invisibly
their blue, conceptual shore.
The chromium was gleaming
on a fisherman's damp bike,
the Phantoms armed and ready for
that night's pre-emptive strike,
as the little torch packed up on us
leaving tides to hush us home
on candlepowered ecologies
and batteries of foam.

A Yard of Chiffon

On winter nights like this she's not at home;
Her dead child coughs and scuffles, knocking chairs,
Comes shining like an untwinned chromosome
In white-glazed tiles down disinfected stairs.
Almost as if they'd woken up next door
The little voices process through the room
And loved ones ride the ether to explore
Damp's bronchial, evaporating bloom.

She's overwrought, her floral dress is soiled,
Her feet stone cold in patent leather shoes,
Her false teeth glow, improbable as pearls,
Each eyelid sunk and lowered like a bruise.
This house of spirits seems quite orthodox,
A semi in a short, tree-muffled close,
But as he speaks the vocal darkness locks
Smoked muscle in a disembodied pose

With faces pulled from lacerated phlegm
And painful sobs of plasma, viscous love,
The faked and torchlit traceries of skin,
A yard of chiffon hijacked by a glove.
He keeps the gauze and latex out of mind
In freezer bags and sealed black plastic sacks
Dumped in the loft like corpses left behind
Each evening when the dead have turned their backs.

Pricking the Violet

The vestry filled with umbilical light,
two forty-watt bulbs, charred tendons of flex,
the ruined, hepatic tinge of their trite
shades on the wafer-thin page of the text
    'In the beginning was the Word'
warped by the talkative shadows we threw,
the cheap sash window, its afternoon blurred
by whorls in the retinal ghostings of blue.
Spoon-fed on Jesus we snorted the dust
sifted from decades of prurient kids;
skin cells, illusions, a dandruff of trust
pricking the violet of tightly shut lids.
We scuffed our feet through the magnetized specks
and filed through the gloom to a Sunday tea,
to a News Of The World, the print-smudge of sex
on a white cuff's biblical clarity.

Singeing

The barber's tubes and rubber bulbs,
their wheezing scents, asthmatic talcs,
have long since perished
with the rest of his tribal paraphernalia;
the Brylcreems set in misty jars
and the almost medieval singeing straws,
wax tapers with their red-hot buds
that, smoking, sealed the ends of hairs
and left the neck an acrid stem,
smart meat, a stook of tendons.
They don't go in for singeing now,
hair-triggered, charred against the grain,
the kind of shock reserved for cancers
or to rustle the brain-cells of the clinically depressed;
but once its smell
hung over the entire country,
particularly the short-back-and-sides of Southern England,
and especially in the autumn in the shaved afternoons.
Some still believe it works
and some of those
itch to be able to prophesy its return,
that after the harvest, between smashed street lamps,
they might lift up their heads and smell the stubble burn.

A Cigar

Eleven o'clock. Smoke turns in its lung,
Blue muscles of petrol contract on the air,
At the back of my throat, on the tip of my tongue
Red pores and their needle capillaries flare
As someone calls 'Time' and a door swings to
And showers of fake candescence escape,
Crashed neon adhering like animal glue
To a melt-down of faces, skin's nuclear crêpe.
What's to become of us? Here, all alone,
In this warm, overfurnished corner of space
Where hair and hot perfume upholster the bone
Spun from fortuitous carbon and gas.
Already the shimmering fictions we store,
Their organic paper and vegetable ink,
The recombinant tripe of their metaphor,
Their narrative fibre and lexical bulk,
Prepare for extinction, a pulped self-destruct,
A fuel for tomorrow's deciduous blaze;
Soft acres of pap, whole forestfuls sucked
Down night's astrophysical backalleyways
Towards all these singular, spine-chilling stars
Where light from the future has gone round the bend
And time, like the tip of this gloomy cigar,
Grows brighter and hotter approaching the end.

Airfix

I used to buy a model once a week
With plastic wings on burs attached to sticks.
I very quickly mastered the technique.
A way of killing time for 2/6d.

(At weekends it was something else to do;
Ejector seats, the roundel transfer slips,
Transparent cockpits, surplus films of glue
Like shiny scales beneath my fingertips).

I finished and suspended them from thread
To climb or dive or simulate a swoop,
With one ambitious kit above my bed
Tip-tiltedly prepared to loop-the-loop;

But pretty soon my bedroom had become
An air controller's nightmare, fluff and dust,
The sky above a timeless aerodrome
And waking up a reflex of distrust.

I shelled them with hot pokers and set light
To port and starboard engines, watched them blaze
And smashed them in a parody of flight.
Two dozen hits in half as many days.

They went up like a prayer, a plume of black,
Tiger Moths, Mosquitoes, Yorks and Spits,
And left me with the stench, the lifelong knack
Of posthumously sweeping up the bits.

Love and Kisses

A gold archangel blows four silver doves
Across the frozen surface of the card;
A bruiser's face, two beaten metal gloves,
Unfolded wings cosmetically enlarged:
The effort fills its cheeks out, stings its eyes,
Sends ripples through the cold, imagined air,
Stars feather in an uprush of surprise
Swept spherically around the paper square.

The halo slips its focus, two raised bands
Are held in an impossible ellipse,
The babyface is puffed with golden glands,
Each polished bird ecstatically dips.
And that is all. Simplicity. Pressed fact.
A minor emblematic tour-de-force
Relying for its seasonal impact
On feelings at their unambitious source.

The card is from a cousin now split up
And living with her newly teenage sons,
Still breathless at the springing of the trap
And tensed to see the way their fresh luck runs,
They're happy, or provisionally so.
Inside his missing name creates a glare
And higher up, like bird prints over snow,
Their love and kisses test the chilly air.

Slush

These sagged and granulated days
Grow cellular with sunlit snow
As slush and cradled ice erase
Our little Spring *in utero*;
Expanding nights wheel on the stars
Above the glass and chromium cars,
Their bonnets, boots and roofs embossed
With snorted signatures of frost.

It won't last long, enough perhaps
To fool the crocuses and bring
Deep-frozen squirrels out of wraps
Or trick some thrushes into song;
But while it does sensation bites
On shrilly ventilated skies,
Aerobic blues, anoxic whites
The high-grade winds anaesthetise.

Dusk comes early, as we drive
Onto the slurring motorway
Our spectral wipers just survive
The muck from an exhausted day.
Last night, it seems, you had a show,
The stalled transparencies of blood,
A trail gone cold, a hump of snow
One more bright spell will thaw and flood.

Coconut

He showed me how to tap them, drill the hole
Then hold them upside down so milk could pass
Through chars of cradle-cap around the skull
And pour like misted pee into a glass;
The drink was mine, a cloudy tot, a toast,
Thin sperm shot by some Caribbean ghost.
The hard part was the sharp, wrist-driven blow
That hit the seam and split the shell to show
Internal shards, their collars of strict light
And flaming tufts of beard pre-Raphaelite.
Inside the husk the pucker on the skin
Was soaped and shrivelled, rucked by formalin,
The fibrous clench of cleanness underneath
A mock ceramic whiter than our teeth.

I shared an old man's relish, packing up
A canteen of scooped wood on either knee,
Organic saucers, shallows of wigged cup,
Our wizened, neolithic crockery.
I saw his cleaned-up corpse three days before
His wooden trundle through the furnace door;
Close-shaven, washed and waxed, the nasal hair
Trimmed back but silver, visible, his stare
Closed down with the expression on his face,
A chemical, deracinated grace.
Some ginger hairs still spiralled from his wrist
Above the hand that wrapped my shaky fist
And taught me how to hit and what it means,
Who missed or smashed his shells to smithereens.

A Different Fireside

Schists and micas, fractal, absolute blacks,
Lucifer's hoof-clippings picketing light,
Pulverized forests, cathedrals in sacks,
Dead hundredweights of blue Jurassic night
Tipped down the coal-hole with haloes of dust,
Coronas of carbon, atomised thorn,
A tart, prehistoric, lung-shrinking gust,
The nationalized breath of the unicorn.

This was our fuel for six months of the year.
My run with the scuttle and difficult tongs,
Night's carboniferous passage of fear,
The wide-eyed canaries' terminal songs.
Much later, sitting in front of the fire
Watching deciduous gases escape,
The galleried ash collapse and aspire,
A cat's eye peel like a luminous grape,

The ghosts in the cellar seemed banished for good,
Cambrian demons put back in their box;
Bad dreams, a neanderthal Birnam Wood
Safe under archaeological locks.
The clash between the miners and police
Came later, by a different fireside;
The fission of cameras as flashes released
A blaze of upturned faces petrified.

A Clean Shave

A curve of pinholed foil protects
Tough semicircles, Iron Age blades
All honed for more resilient necks
And jaws than mine; a livered brown
Collecting where the brightness fades
Along the sprung, old-fangled crown.

He'd had this razor fifteen years.
A birthday present, rarely used,
Preferring, as he did, thin blears
Of soap and water, strop and blade.
The three staff nurses all refused.
A compromise, it seems, was made.

I lift the heads, surprised to find
A puff of stubble and dead skin,
The troughs of moulded plastic lined
With white cutaneous dust I kissed
And fall-out from the lips and chin
That from today do not exist.

After death the hairs still grow,
Nails lengthen pinkly in the earth
And bristles leave their grey velcro
On faces as the cheeks decay.
I sift and tilt this peck of scurf
Then blow the last of him away

And plug it in to shave and find
The heat revives his acrid smell
As though there's something left behind
Long after all the muffed goodbyes
And every hair and scattered cell
To justify the compromise.

Early Warning

If you were a nuclear superpower
And I were a buffer state
I'd cling like dirt to your arable skirt
Where the Cruise proliferate,
And my Early Warning system
Would mesh with the nerve ends of yours
And your arms would keep the peace while I sleep
And colonize the stars;
I would launder inflationary taxes
And absorb your acid rain
Though each river and stream might audibly scream
With the ecological pain.

If you were an overgrown continent
And I were a bit on the side
I would love to explore your coastal floor
And the plains where your prairies ride.
I would hoover your latest missiles
And polish the stainless steel screens
Where titanium fits like silicone tits
On the tops of your submarines;
And at the United Nations,
Alone in the hullabaloo,
Despite the disgrace and the loss of face
I would always vote for you.

Or if I were the dominant planet
And you were my satellite
I would let you pass through my volatile gas
And spin you through the night:
I would catch and recycle your atoms
And cherish your orbit and shape
The darkened half of your crooked path
To speed up your escape,
And then dance you across the heavens
And blister the firmament
And the stars would uncross at whatever the cost
Until our love was spent.

If I were as rich as you're pretty
Or you were as small as I'm poor
Our hands might have stopped the glandular clock
And the hormonal calendar
Where the season was always autumn
And the weather in bad repair,
Trust hung by a thread and the lights went dead
In your eyes and your blinding hair
As I looked for a private conclusion
Or an easier way to choke
On the gorgeous mess of its loveliness
Before the morning broke.

Soundtrack

Dusk settles on the beach, one winter star
Flints sharp and white, a Stone Age solitary,
As wall to wall in night's cold cinema
Waves play their endless soundtrack to the sea;
Tides frisk the rock pools, gargle baby crabs,
Snort foam and sewage, chemical soft-soap,
Then something more, a radiance that stabs,
The afterlife of some rogue isotope.
It comes in from the East with poisoned fish,
Frail, pink-rinsed crustaceans, empty shells,
Slips underneath the whiskered radar dish
With news of melt-downs, fireballs, sickle-cells.
The sea, Time's numbercruncher, goes haywire,
Shakes limestone to its fossil-haunted quick;
The Music of the Spheres, the Heavenly Choir
Are gravelled by its bass *realpolitik*.
A flask of mirrored windows runs to ground
The asphalt road that threads our glass estate,
Built on the shining bones of all the drowned
We hover where the stars disintegrate.
What's coming round is still light-years away
Re-routed through the West's smart microchips,
Atlantis, Xanadu, Moscow, Pompeii,
Earth's neon-tripped, flashlit apocalypse.
What will these crabs inherit when we run?
Boiled foreshores stippled by an acrid rain,
The mauve blink of an ultra-violet sun
That microwaves our silos of snuffed grain,
The insects' silver wiring in the fields,
Blue dawns of static, mooned acetylene,
The lead-lined bunker killing what it shields
Behind the punched-out vacuum of the screen.

Mascara

Your lashes shed their urban loads,
Puffed clots and inartistic smears
Like beauty's skid-marks, toxic roads,
Red lights and poisoned atmospheres,
While under lids specific veins
Reveal their intravenous weight
In floating bruises, shellacked stains
Old powders still adulterate.
Daybreak, the quirky crow long gone
That prints its subcutaneous seams
On pulsing smuts of skin and bone
In fat's apocalyptic dreams.
How complicated life's become,
Your physiology, your white,
Hormonally upholstered womb
That keeps our baby watertight;
The lucid damage as you wake
Among synthetic blots and curves
And tears that smudge and speck and cake
These blackspots where the morning swerves.

Vacuum

I came back from the hospital half-stoned
and brushed against your plastic flask
caught cold in a tubular moonlight
falling through a haze of frosted glass.
I stood and watched its wobble of reproach,
the stem of the vacuum silver with absence,
its clinical brightness darkened by tea;
old tensions and
their watermarked fragility
sterilized and shrinking from my touch.

The tube broke with an atmospheric crunch.
I picked it up and shook it.
The noise it made was the same as the sea's
splintered at the chalk foot of a cliff;
a shining insulation,
the mirrored hiss
as microscopic voices seethed
with still-born cries
and, running through my fingers, were released.

X-Ray

A pearl bulb floods what's left of life,
Its lifted rib-cage streams with light,
The latch of each candescent tooth
Shut on the darkness of your bite;
Its milky, ultra-violet spine
Occluded by a cloudy lung
And, rooted in the skull's blind shine,
The swallowed shadow of your tongue.

These cameras dispense with skin,
Wipe out smudged lipstick, sweat, cologne,
Come down on you and zero in
On deep, illuminated bone,
Ignoring what I thought was real,
Flared nostrils, make-up's high-pitched bloom,
Your instep's rucked, elastic chill,
Tubed breasts and ointments, stale perfume.

They filed your case-notes when you died,
Red ink, sun-faded carbons, tape,
This exposed plate slipped half inside
A tied and humped manilla shape;
Out of the black and unlit blue
Your faint bones glimmer, pale, ill-starred,
Their ghostly edges breaking through
The dog-ears of your record-card.